THE BUSINESS]
BLUEPRINT

By: Tearod Robertson

T. Robertson Publishing, Co.
Copyright © 2015
ISBN (978-0-9888-144-3-1)

TABLE OF CONTENTS

Page 03   Inroduction

Page 08   What is Your Vision

Page 09   What's on Your Bucket List

Page 10   The Formula for Passion

Page 11   Executive Summary

Page 14   Company Description

Page 17   Market Analysis

Page 24   Organization & Management

Page 25   Ownership Information

Page 48   Board of Directors Qualifications

Page 54   Service or Product Line

Page 57   Marketing & Sales

Page 60   Financials

Page 71   Appendix

Page 72   Business Consultants

Page 75   The D.E.A.M. Approach

INTRODUCTION

This book is designed as a supplement to my book The D.E.A.M. Approach Effectively Marketing to Build Business. If you do not have a copy already, I strongly recommend it. You will find it very valuable as pieces of that book, are introduced beginning on page 75 of this book.

In the D.E.A.M. Approach, I outline strategies of creating marketing plans to help propel your business to the next level. In outlining those strategies I give costs associated with each of those strategies to help you gain some sort of idea of what is real for you to accomplish within the budget you have.

By creating a budget for marketing, you are able to forecasts sales and marketing needs, giving you a clearer picture of finances needed to launch or revamp your business.

This book (Blueprint) will help you build a more defined model of your business as you create your business plan. Take your time and think about the descriptions of items that you create on the following pages . Really place some thought and research into the cost that you place on line items. If you do this, you will find that you will have created a very thorough business plan for you to build your business, or increase the sales of your current business.

However, remember plans are meant to be broken. You will find as you grow your business that you will have to make adjustments on thoughts, principles and costs from time to time. That is O.K. It is what I call " business growth." Just understand when you are undergoing business growth verses "just not following the business plan."

Not following the business plan is, most times, worse than not having a plan at all.

With that noted, you should in fact revisit your business plan every nine months. I like this formula because it allows you to tackle your business for three quarters out of the year, assess needs for change and make those changes to prepare for implementation the last quarter. It also allows for you to revisit the plan once every other year and, twice the years in between.

This is a very aggressive business strategy. It is good for small businesses that are witnessing exponential growth and finding a need to maintain stability while growing, not losing control and revamping budgets and projections to reflect such growth.

So, enjoy this book. But, more importantly utilize it to your maximum capacity. By creating the model for your business systems within the framework of this book, you are in route to increasing sales, turning your dream into a reality or providing the bank with what is needed to get that business loan.

WHAT IS YOUR VISION?

Your vision is the legacy you want to create, and leave for your business and your family.

_____

_____

_____

_____

_____

_____

WHAT'S ON YOUR BUCKET LIST?

We all have things that we want to do and places that we want to go. We say we would do them if had just a little more time, or just a little more money.

Things to Do

Places to Go

_____ _____

_____ _____

_____ _____

_____ _____

_____ _____

_____ _____

_____ _____

_____ _____

> *There are two or three things that we will do. No matter how difficult the task or, how time consuming they may be, we do them because we just like to do them. This is for what we have passion.*

The Formula for PASSION

What You Like to Do + What You Will do for Free = PASSION

What do I Like to Do + Will I do for Free = Do I have passion?
  (Yes/No)   (Yes / No)   (Yes / No)

_____   _____   _____

_____   _____   _____

_____   _____   _____

_____   _____   _____

_____   _____   _____

_____   _____   _____

EXECUTIVE SUMMARY

Your executive summary outlines the pertinent information and details about your company. If someone wants to know what your business is about, they should be able to find this information in your executive summary.

✦ MISSION STATEMENT

_____

_____

_____

_____

_____

✦ COMPANY INFORMATION

_____

_____

✦ GROWTH HIGHLIGHTS

_____

_____

_____

_____

_____

✦ YOUR PRODUCTS AND SERVICES

_____

_____

_____

_____

_____

✦ FINANCIAL INFORMATION

_____

_____

_____

_____

_____

✦ SUMMARIZE FUTURE PLANS

_____

_____

_____

_____

_____

_____

_____

COMPANY DESCRIPTION

Who is your company? What product or services does your company provide? These questions give the description of your business.

✦ DESCRIBE NATURE OF BUSINESS

_____

_____

_____

_____

_____

_____

_____

✦ EXPLAIN HOW YOUR PRODUCTS AND SERVICES MEET NEEDS

+ List specific consumers to be served

_____

_____

_____

_____

_____

_____

+ Explain competitive advantage

_____

_____

_____

_____

_____

MARKET ANALYSIS

Your market is your customer base. You should get to know your market; who they are, where they are, and how you can win their business over the competition.

+ Industry description and outlook

_____

_____

_____

_____

_____

+ Target Market

_____

_____

_____

_____

_____

+ Distinguishing characteristics

_____

_____

_____

_____

_____

+ Size of Target Market

_____

_____

_____

_____

+ How much of market can you gain

_____

_____

_____

_____

_____

+ Pricing and gross margin targets

_____

_____

_____

_____

_____

Competitive Analysis

Get to know your competition. Know what Their doing, and who are their customers.

- Market Share

_____

_____

_____

_____

_____

- Strengths and Weaknesses

_____

_____

_____

- Importance of Target Market to Competition

_____

_____

_____

_____

- What is your window of opportunity

_____

_____

_____

_____

_____

_____

_____

- Secondary competitors

_____

_____

_____

_____

- Barriers to enter the market

_____

_____

_____

_____

_____

✦ Regulatory Restrictions

ORGANIZATION & MANAGEMENT

Creating a strong since that you understand your organization and its management style will not only increase your depth of your businesses' perception, it will also increase the depth of perception of potential investors.

Organizational Structure

_____

_____

_____

_____

_____

_____

_____

OWNERSHIP INFORMATION

> *Investors, banks and even your customers want to know who are the owners Of the company.*

Owner Name

_____

Percentage of Ownership

_____

Forms of ownership

_____

Outstanding equity

_____

Common Stock Shares Owned

_____

MANAGEMENT PROFILES

Who are your officers?

President

Name

_____

Responsibilities

_____

_____

_____

_____

_____

Education

_____

Experience / Skills

_____

_____

_____

_____

Prior Employment

_____

_____

_____

_____

_____

Special Skills

_____

_____

_____

_____

_____

Past track record

_____

_____

_____

_____

_____

_____

Industry recognition

_____

_____

_____

_____

_____

Community Involvement

_____

_____

_____

_____

_____

Number of years with company

_____

Compensation basis levels

- Quantify achievements

Resume (Insert Here)

Vice-President

Name

_____

Responsibilities

_____

_____

_____

_____

_____

Education

_____

_____

_____

Experience / Skills

_____

_____

_____

_____

_____

Prior Employment

_____

Special Skills

_____

_____

_____

_____

_____

Past track record

_____

_____

_____

_____

_____

Industry recognition

_____

_____

_____

_____

_____

_____

Community Involvement

_____

_____

_____

_____

_____

Number of years with company

_____

Compensation basis levels

_____

_____

_____

_____

_____

- Quantify achievements

_____

_____

_____

_____

_____

_____

_____

_____

_____

_____

_____

Resume (Insert Here)

Treasurer

Name

_____

Responsibilities

_____

_____

_____

_____

_____

Education

_____

_____

_____

Experience / Skills

_____

_____

_____

_____

_____

Prior Employment

_____

Special Skills

_____

Past track record

_____

_____

_____

Industry recognition

_____

Community Involvement

_____

_____

_____

_____

_____

Number of years with company

_____

Compensation basis levels

_____

_____

+ Quantify achievements

Resume (Insert Here)

Secretary

Name

_____

Responsibilities

_____

_____

_____

_____

Education

_____

_____

_____

_____

Experience / Skills

_____

_____

_____

_____

_____

Prior Employment

_____

Special Skills

_____

Past track record

_____

_____

_____

_____

Industry recognition

_____

_____

_____

_____

_____

Community Involvement

_____

_____

_____

_____

_____

Number of years with company

_____

Compensation basis levels

_____

_____

_____

_____

_____

• Quantify achievements

_____

_____

_____

_____

_____

Resume (Insert Here)

Board of Directors Qualifications

> You should recruit a board of directors that will be honest with you and hold you accountable for making decisions for the good of the company.

Board Member #1

_____

Position of Board

_____

Extent of company involvement

_____

_____

_____

Background

_____

_____

_____

_____

_____

Historical and future contribution of success

_____

_____

_____

_____

_____

_____

Board Member #2

_____

Position of Board

_____

Extent of company involvement

_____

_____

_____

Background

_____

_____

_____

Historical and future contribution of success

_____

_____

_____

_____

_____

_____

_____

_____

_____

_____

Board Member #3

_____

Position of Board

_____

Extent of company involvement

_____

_____

_____

Background

_____

_____

_____

_____

_____

Historical and future contribution of success

SERVICE OR PRODUCT LINE

Whether you are providing a service or selling a widget, you must know how to determine its value. This includes everything from manufacturing to the amount of hours you spend with a client.

DESCRIPTION OF SERVICE / PRODUCT

_____

_____

_____

_____

_____

_____

_____

DETAIL PRODUCT LIFE CYCLE

_____

_____

_____

_____

INTELLECTUAL PROPERTY

_____

_____

_____

_____

RESEARCH AND DEVELOPMENT ACTIVITIES

MARKETING & SALES

MARKET PENETRATION STRATEGY

_____

_____

_____

_____

_____

_____

_____

_____

_____

_____

FINANCIAL DATA

Banks and investors are all about the numbers. The more financial data you can provide, the better will assist your case in getting funding.

1. BREAK EVEN ANALYSIS

BREAK Even   = $\dfrac{\text{Fixed Costs} / 1\text{- Variable Costs per Unit}}{\text{Selling price per unit}}$

2. HISTORICAL FINANCIAL PROJECTIONS

3. PROSPECTIVE FINANCIAL DATA

Your balance sheet is a snap shot of your current assets (things you own and, liabilities (bills you owe as of right now).

BALANCE SHEET FOR MONTH ENDING JANUARY 2015

Assets		Liabilities and Shareholders' Equity	
Cuurent Assets		Current Liabilities	
Cash and Cash Equivalents		Commercial Paper	
Receivables		Accounts Payable	
Inventories		Accrued Liabilities	
Prepaid Expenses		Accrued Income Taxes	
Total Current Assets		Long Term Debt due within one year	
		Total Current Liabilities	
Property and Equipment			
Land			
Building and Improvements		Long Term Debt due within one year	
Fixtures and Equipment		Long Term Obligations under Capital Leases	
Transportation Equipment		Deferred Income Taxes and other	
Total Property and Equipment		Minority Interest	
Less Accumulated Depreciated		Shareholders Equity:	
Property and Equipment		Preferred Stock	
		Common Stock	
Property under Capital Lease		Capital in Excess of Par Value	

62

Goodwill		Accumulated other Comprehensive Income	
Other Assets and Deferred Charges		Retained Earnings	
		Total Shareholders' Equity	
Total Assets		**Total Liabilities and Shareholders Equity**	

Balance Sheet Continued

Your pro-forma is merely your forecasted revenues and projections. You should create a pro-forma that shows three years of projections.

BUSINESS PRO-FORMA 2015

Revenenues:	
Net Sales	
Interest Income	
Gains from Sale of Fixed or Non-Current Assets	
Total Revenues	
Cost and Expenses	
Cost of Goods Sold	
Salaries	
Office or Store Supplies	
Repairs & Maintenance	
Utilities (Power, Water, Phone)	
Insurance Expense	
Interest Expense	

Rent Expenses	
Taxes and Licenses	
Advertising Expenses	
Transportation & Traveling	
Depreciation Expenses	
Total Costs & Expenses	
Net Income / (Net Loss)	

Pro-forma Continued

GROWTH STRATEGY

_____

_____

_____

_____

_____

CHANNELS OF DISTRIBUTION STRATEGY

_____

_____

_____

_____

_____

COMMUNICATION STRATEGY

_____

_____

_____

_____

_____

SALES STRATEGY

_____

_____

_____

_____

SALES FORCE STRATEGY

_____

_____

_____

_____

_____

SALES ACTIVITIES

_____

_____

_____

_____

_____

FUNDING REQUEST

If you are going to require a business loan or investment dollars, you should be prepared to be extremely transparent as to how funds will be used.

CURRENT FUNDING REQUIREMENT

_____

_____

_____

_____

_____

✦ HOW YOU INTEND TO USE THE FUNDS

_____

_____

_____

_____

═══════════════════════════════

+ ANY STRATEGIC FINANCIAL SITUATIONS

_____

_____

_____

_____

_____

+ FUTURE FUNDING REQUIREMENTS FOR
NEXT FIVE YEARS

_____

_____

_____

_____

APPENDIX

Product Pictures

Reumes of Key Managers

LETTER OF REFERENCE 1

LETTER OF REFERENCE 2

LETTER OF REFERENCE 1

MARKET STUDY DETAILS

MAGAZINE ARTICLES AND BOOK
REFERENCES

COPY OF LICENSES

COPY OF BUILDING PERMITS

COPY OF CONTRACTS

BUSINESS CONSULTANTS

Attorney's Name

_____

Attorney's Phone Number

_____

Attorney's Address

_____

CPA's Name

_____

CPA's Phone Number

_____

CPA's Address

_____

Other Consultant

_____

Phone Number

_____

Address

_____

Other Consultant

_____

Phone Number

_____

Address

_____

THE DEAM APPROACH

This section of the book is dedicated to growing your business thru marketing. you can find the more detailed information on marketing in my Book: The D.E.A.M. Approach.

Personal Contact Marketing - List 10 friends / family from your contact data base.

1. _____

2. _____

3. _____

4. _____

5. _____

6. _____

7. _____

8. _____

Social Media Marketing - List your social media

1. _____

2. _____

3. _____

4. _____

5. _____

6. _____

7. _____

8. _____

9. _____

10. _____

E-Mail Marketing - List your Top-10 email contacts

1. _____

2. _____

3. _____

4. _____

5. _____

6. _____

7. _____

8. _____

9. _____

10. _____

Text Message Marketing - List your Top-10 email contacts

1. _____

2. _____

3. _____

4. _____

5. _____

6. _____

7. _____

8. _____

9. _____

10. _____

Web-Site Marketing -

_____

_____

_____

_____

_____

Pay Per Click (PPC) Marketing - List five key-words which you would like to use to advertise

1. _____

2. _____

3. _____

4. _____

5. _____

* **Radio Advertising** - List five radio stations on which you would like to advertise

    1. _____

    2. _____

    3. _____

    4. _____

    5. _____

* **Magazine Advertising** - List five magazines in which you would like to advertise

    1. _____

    2. _____

    3. _____

    4. _____

    5. _____

+ **Community and Social Newspaper Advertising** - List five social / community newspapers in which you would like to advertise

1. _____

2. _____

3. _____

4. _____

5. _____

List your total projected monthly revenues

January   _____

February   _____

March   _____

April   _____

May   _____

June   _____

July   _____

August   _____

September   _____

October   _____

November   _____

December   _____

Marketing expenses - List marketing expenses and projected cost (3.5% of total revenue)

- **Grass Roots**

    1. _____

    2. _____

    3. _____

    4. _____

    5. _____

- **Print**

    1. _____

    2. _____

    3. _____

    4. _____

    5. _____

✦ Internet

1. _____

2. _____

3. _____

4. _____

5. _____

PRESENTATION

I hope this book was able to help you better organize your thoughts as you completed each item of your business plan.

Now all you have to do is take the outline that you have used here, to create your business plan, and reproduce it in a soft copy.

What we have not discussed to this point is the final presentation. Once you create the soft copy of your business plan, you should then print the hard copy, and insert section dividers at each topic. Use the Table of Contents of this book to determine your sections.

You should also have the hard copy professionally bound by a local copy or print company. I like to always make copies in threes. I also like spiral binding, as opposed to coil binding.

By having three copies, you can put one on your book shelf for future reference. You can give one to be proofed by a team member to be marked up and, you will have one that you can mark-up yourself. Your business plan can easily be fifty pages. Spiral binding will make it easy for you to read thru and turn the pages of such a document.

Oh yeah, don't forget to make sure that you have your page numbering set to on. I like my page numbers in the lower right corner.

Just remember that a good business plan is one that is a work-in-progress. How often you revisit your business plan, is a good indicator of the growth of your business.

Good luck on building your business!!!

OTHER TITLES BY THE AUTHOR

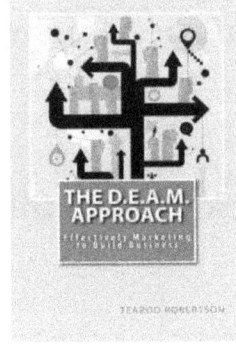

1. The Best Idea I Ever Had Right Now!!!

2. The Best Idea I Ever Had Right Now!!! (The Pink Copy)

3. The D.E.A.M. Approach -Effectively Marketing to Build Business

Author Contact Info:

www.TearodRobertson.com

Facebook.com/TearodRobertson

Instagram: @TearodR

Twitter: @TearodR

www.ingramcontent.com/pod-product-compliance
Lightning Source LLC
Chambersburg PA
CBHW020210200326
41521CB00005BA/329